# indigo
# spirals

# Indigo Spirals

## Pathways to Wisdom

### Virginnia Radford

ATHENA PRESS
LONDON

ISBN 978 1 84748 726 1

First published 2010 by
ATHENA PRESS
Queen's House, 2 Holly Road
Twickenham TW1 4EG
United Kingdom

Printed and bound in Great Britain by CPI Antony Rowe,
Chippenham and Eastbourne

Printed for Athena Press

Life is good
Life is bad
But Life is Beautiful
(Mari)

When Life becomes tough,
enjoy the challenges it brings.

Within every problem,
heartache,
frustration,
and pain

there is the beautiful opportunity
of uncovering a great Gift:

that of re-Remembering
Who you Really Are.

Life is Beautiful

Within every human action,
whatever its outward appearance,
lies a hidden Spirit,
an Essence of Beauty.

Courage and a determination
to rise above
and conquer
fear, once and for all,
stirs
and intensifies
within the Heart
of any victim of fear-laden
aggression or submission...

Your Heart
demands Truth and Purity.

Fear has no place
outside the mind...

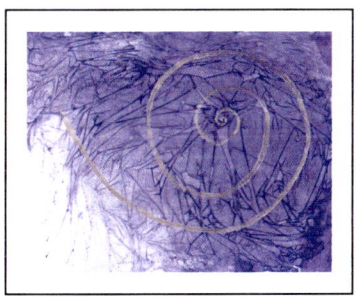

Fear
denies the existence of
Love,
Wisdom,
Compassion,
Forgiveness,
Generosity of Spirit...

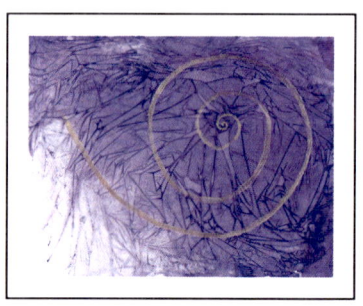

So fight
the self-degradation
and sense of
Powerlessness
that fear generates.

Fight for that which is of the
Heart,
which shows you the Truth
that

Life is Beautiful

Love the innocence
of a child as he raises his eyes
to meet yours.

Know that you would challenge
anyone
who would take that away from him.

## Life is Beautiful

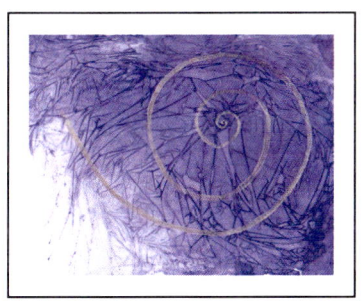

Love the smile
given to you by your Lover
as you awaken entwined in their arms.

## Life is Beautiful

Love the simplest of things:

The diamond points of light sparkling
on a cobweb,
touched by the golden rays
of an early morning sun,
shimmering in the clearing mists
of an awakening autumn day.

# Life is Beautiful

☺

Love
the manifested Beauty
revealed in Nature.

Accept and allow its Perfection,
without
Judgement
or desire
to change it
into something that it is not.

# Life is Beautiful

Know
that the Hand of the Divine Creator
is at Work
within all experience.

To see
how one's own Creative Design
has manifested each
personal experience
is

True Understanding...

To then
take that Understanding
into a new,
fresh,
simpler
and purer Experience is...

Wisdom...

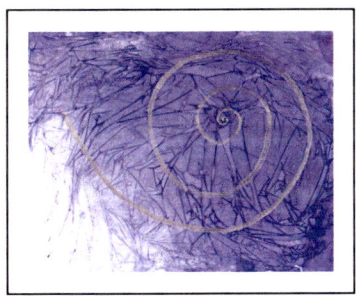

Wisdom...
is how you use the knowledge
that you all have

for the greatest good of all...

To be Wise is to be a Master:
to be _in_ the world
but
Not _of_ the world...

# Life is simple.

We make Life complicated
so we can understand it.

As we come to understand Life,
it becomes simpler
and
simpler.

# Life is Beautiful

The Divine Creator
only creates that which is Beautiful.

We of the Earth create Beauty
all the time
when we allow
our Heart's passionate Voice
to guide us.
It is through our Heart that the Divine
speaks and has expression.
There is so much incredible, awesome,
amazing Beauty in what we do
when we
remember that...

Life is Beautiful

All Creation
Comes from one Divine Source,
whatever our own name
for this Power.

We are all made from
identical Fragments
of that Divine Energy.

We are truly One with
All Creation...

All these fragments
contain within them the Essence,
the Blueprint, of the Divine Source.

All are thereby linked,
ultimately,
to the One.

Each fragment is a Beautiful,
Unique
Aspect of the One.

The Beauty of the Divine One
created us
and...

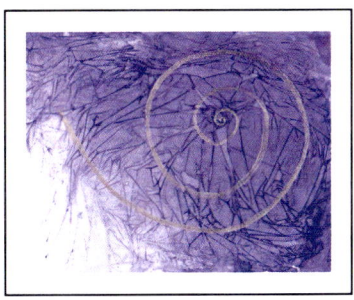

Our Earthly Journey

is very much composed
of taking Paths
that allow us to understand
the physical ego...

...that of the 'I'...

☺

All the time

our Spirit –
our essential,
Divine Self –
guides us
towards the Spiritual Ego

...that of...

'I AM!'...

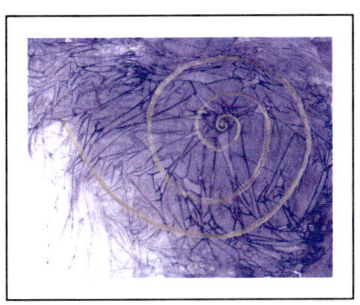

When we can stand naked
and shout...

I AM!

to the world
and the Universe,
we come Home,
at last,
to our Selves...

Who we Really Are...

As we arrive Home,

we can look back on our long Journeying
and truly

Know

that all our experiences along the way
have held the gifts of Beauty within them.

We can then truly say, with Love,
Understanding
and Wisdom...

Life is Beautiful

Here, as physical beings,

we can only see the full Power,
the profundity, of Beauty
when we can see
how it has been uglified.

To repair, rebuild, to reshape
that which we have tarnished and uglified
is to reveal something in ourselves
that has even greater beauty...

In doing this we reveal,
complement and expand
the Beauty that is our true being...
Our Divine Essence.

We also fulfil our promise to the
Divine One...
that of evolving into the amazing, gifted,
wonder-full, unique Beings that the
Divine One intended us to be.

At completion of one incarnate journeying
we can stand Tall
and truly understand and Know that...

Life is Beautiful

Believe in yourself!

(why not?)...

You
express that Beautiful Being deep
within you
when you are Creative.

Love all that you do, however mundane
and commonplace,
for it gladdens your eyes
and enriches your mind
and Heart...

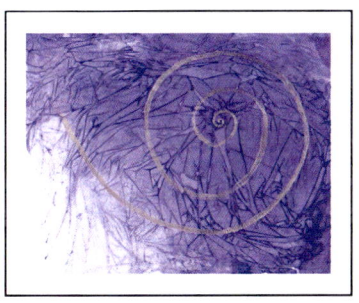

Being creative
can be when you paint,
compose a song
or write a letter...

Read a story
to a child

or take a friend to watch the beauty
of a wind-blown sky
or sit with them and share
their joy at a special event
or watch the way cloud shadows
stroke a colour-drenched landscape.

All these are as creatively valid,
significant
and special
as any great artistic masterpiece...

We are all different and special.

We are all born creative.

This gift is never lost,

only diminished
or hidden,
through a belief
that we
are inadequate
or inept...

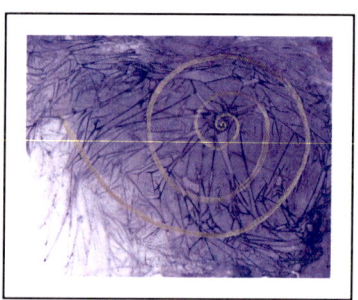

We are all uniquely gifted

in so many

different ways…

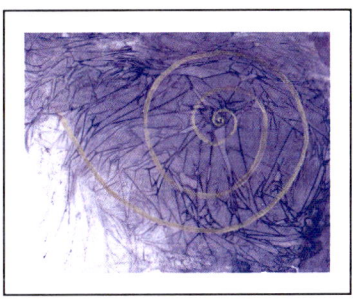

Every one of us,
just by allowing our own creativity
to be expressed,
enriches everything and everyone.

Allow everything that you feel,
think or do
to be filled with Beauty.

Life is Beautiful

Be accountable

For what you create

and reveal yourself to the

world...

As a visitor to this Planet,

Treat it as a treasured home

For the short while you are here...

☺

Honour and care for the Planet.

Do what you can to leave it better
than it was when you arrived.

All Life is Beautiful
and is a fragment of the Divine.

Be accountable for how you care
for all life forms that cannot speak for
or help
themselves.

Life is Beautiful

Be accountable
for the promises you make,
contracts that you enter into
and for the results of all
your actions.

Everything that you experience
is created by


You...


☉


When it comes to Responsibility...
your most fundamental and eternal
Responsibility is for
Yourself.

It is only You
who walks your Earthly Path –
albeit that you will walk alongside
many others
going in the same direction
at different times in your Life...

Everything
that you do is through
your choice...

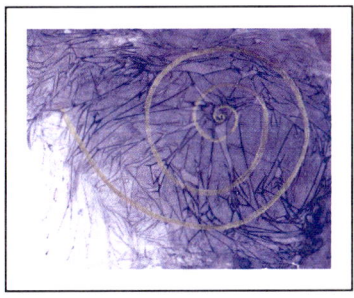

Remember,
All the time, that...

no one makes you
happy,
miserable,
angry,
frustrated...

This is how you
choose
to be...

To React
is the product of the fearful mind.

It can only operate in the past –
from past information,
patterns,
habits
and experience...

๑

To Respond
comes from the Heart.

Listening to your Heart's Voice
and acting upon its prompting
is to hear the Purity of Truth
Revealing, perfectly
and accurately,

just how things Really Are...

Your Heart's Voice

comes direct from your Spirit –
which totally bypasses
the blind illusions
of the mind...

☺

Once you Realise

the difference between
React and
Respond,
then
you can understand that
in
Every Moment...

Life is Beautiful

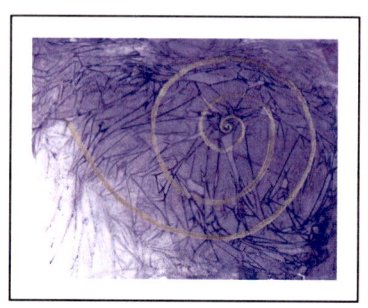

Every word

You say is your responsibility...

As are the consequences
of
those words...

Powerful
and significant energy
is released into the world,

generated by every thought
and feeling
that you have,

and through every word
that you
speak...

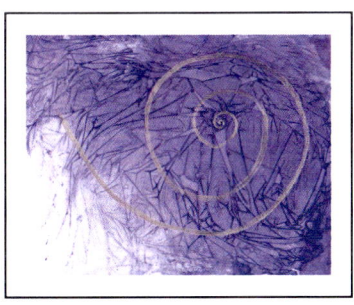

Just consider

What you can achieve
and create
through being responsible for
everything you
say and do!

Then you will begin to see
just how

Life is Beautiful

Honour and Cherish Life –

Yours as well as any other...

☉

Nurture, Nourish
and Sustain Life
within your Body,

as your body is a Gift
lent to you from the Elements,
that your Consciousness helped shape
so that you can
be here...

☉

Everything
on this Planet has a
Consciousness
that gave it form.

All matter, all consciousness,
was created Perfect.

You are Perfect!

Life is Beautiful

# Why do You
constantly beat yourself up
thinking and worrying
about things you have done?

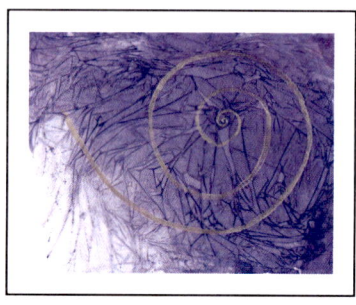

# Why do You
judge them as being bad,
unhelpful,
or see them as mistakes?

You may have hurt someone
unintentionally,
but you still agonise
about the other's pain...

Their reaction
comes solely
from their own perception
– their own take –
of what has happened.

That is their responsibility...

Not Yours...

☉

Remember...

You are not responsible for
another's reaction...

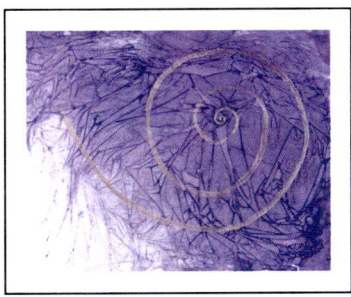

You

have behaved, in that moment,
Perfectly
for where you were at that time
in your understanding
of yourself
and the world around you...

◎

Your Responsibility

is to see your part in the event
and
see how you could have dealt with it
in a more
Loving and Caring way...

# Take Responsibility!

Look at your own fears
and sense of self-worth,
which are behind your thoughts
and behaviour,

and

then change
that which is not worthy of you
for the future...

☺

In every moment, you do your best!

So, in that light,
you have dealt with each moment perfectly.

Therefore,
there cannot be any mistakes...

You have simply been
Exploring
Life.

Always know that whatever
you experience,
however it feels...

Life is Beautiful

ᕲ

Enjoy life!

Have fun!...

Life is Beautiful

ᕲ

Entertain!

Enjoy being entertained!

Life is Beautiful

Enjoy

the

Entertainment

that

Life offers you...

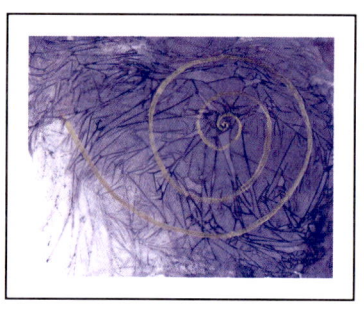

Share your gifts!

All of you

have the fabulous gifts of

Laughter

and

Humour...

Joyous Laughter

raises the vibration in any situation.

Laughter and Humour cheer and soothe
frustration.

They can comfort and heal,
and
bring joy and fun into the world.

Sing out Loud!...

Life is Beautiful

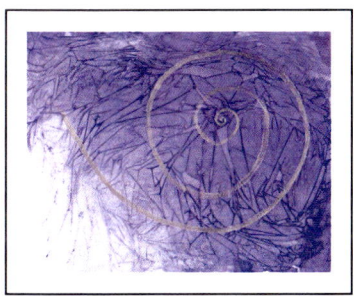

Positive entertainment

encourages
personal growth,
emotional maturity
and self-discipline.

So enjoy everything
that Life offers you, for
the Earth really is
a Playground for all of us!
Draw in the sand...

Life is Beautiful

Explore Life!

Discover more about yourself!

Expand your individuality!...

⊚

You are here

to translate the vast Knowledge
that you have as a Spiritual Being
into Wisdom.

In living Life to the full,

you soon come to realise that

Life is Beautiful

You have chosen
to work with many souls
for the mutual experience of
Discovering
what it is to be
human...

◎

You are all part of a team,
part of the Collective Consciousness
of this Planet.

This being so,
how you feel,
What you think and
All that you do
Profoundly Affects every aspect of the
Planet's Energy...

◎

All life
has a Right
to be treated with

Dignity and Respect...

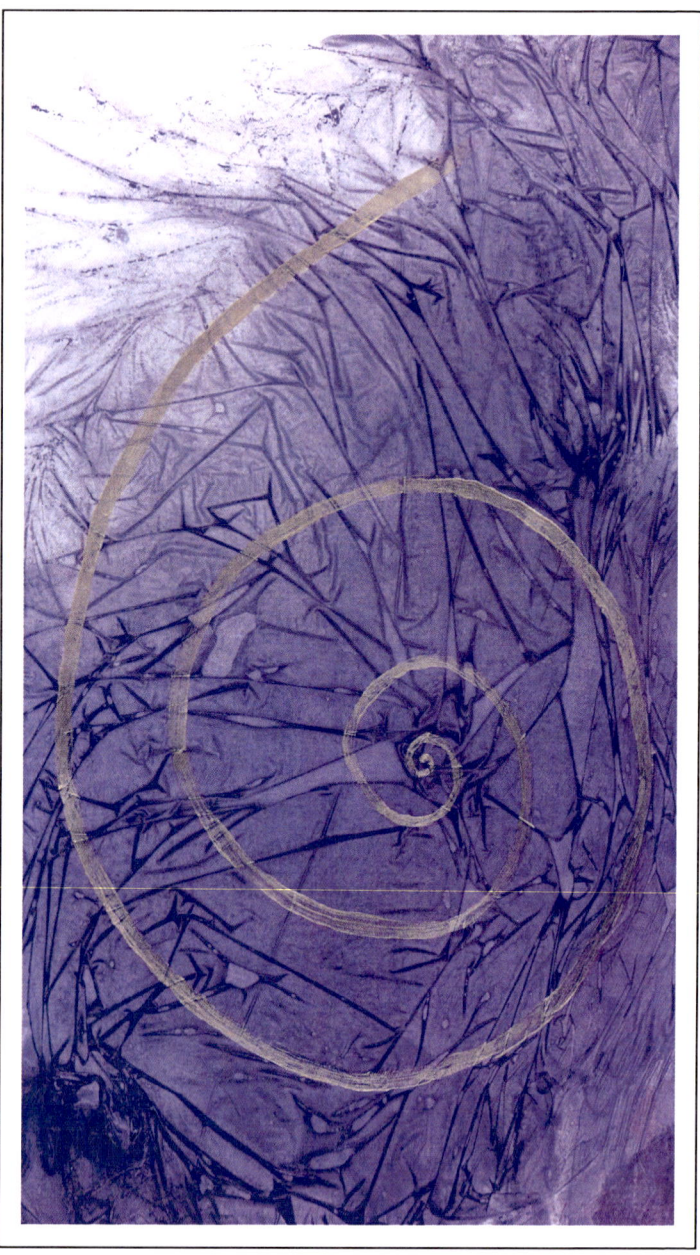

True Service

is caring about others,

sharing knowledge and

contributing something positive

to another's Life...

☺

You are All
so very Special,

Gifted
and Talented,
in so many
different ways.

You are Beautiful

and

# Life is Beautiful

Relationships,
Incidents
and Experiences
are simply

Circles...

๑

There is no difficulty
in closing
every one of your
Circles.

Trust your Heart
and your
Inner Knowing...

Sadness, Frustration,
Anger, Greed,
Guilt, Depression,
Hate, Bitterness,
Anguish...
Are all aspects of Fear.

These are all emotions ruled by the
Mind...

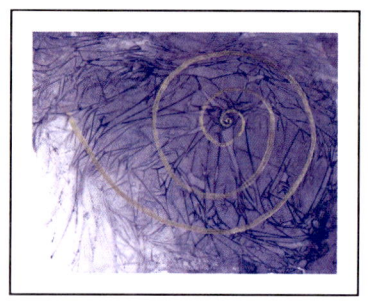

Experience Life
through your
Heart
because
Your Heart
cannot
Know
Fear...

All of us
Are spiritual Beings.
We all come from the same Source.
We are all fragments of the Divine One.

No one is better,
cleverer
or better off

than anyone else...

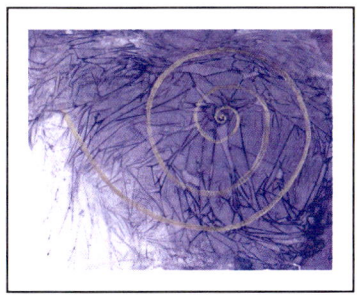

We all stand

shoulder to shoulder with

All Creation,
working together,
unequivocally
Linked together...

We are all created spiritually
perfect.

We continue to be so,
whatever the nature of the path
we choose to follow
on our physical journey...

Life is Beautiful

Every human
is given the same gift:
that of free will,
freedom of choice.
It is this gift that has allowed us
to consider that we
are not Perfect,
so we are prepared to experience
the challenges
that such a belief offers us...

This belief
Allows us to embark fully on the
Adventure
Of acting less than who we really are.

☉

All Life Experiences
are part of that Adventure of Exploration
and self-discovery.
That being so,
all Life is a fabulous Adventure
and as such...

Life is Beautiful

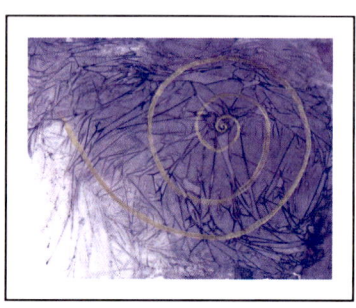

What you Believe in
Exists...

What you do not Believe in
cannot
Exist...

Observe

Without

Judging...

☉

Observe Life

and how it affects you

and how you can learn from that

Observation...

☉

Observe

what is going on
and if it does not feel,
look
or seem right to you
then
Bless it...

And move on...

Release
past experiences,
people
or relationships
in the same way.

All these have come to you
because you have
demanded it
for your current
Journey of Exploration...

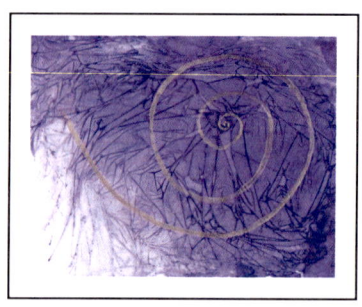

Bless
them all
and let them go,
Knowing that you have received
a special gift from them all,
however it may have appeared
or felt
at the time...

☉

To Observe without Judgement
Allows you to
Understand that all is
in Divine Order

and that we are truly being

in the world

and not of the world...

To Observe without Judgement
is called
'Unconditional Love'.

You put no energy into judging someone
as being wrong.
You have understood
that all involved were, and are,
doing the best they can in that moment.
They are all exploring life.

Just as you are...

If you Judge,

then you must also learn to

Forgive...

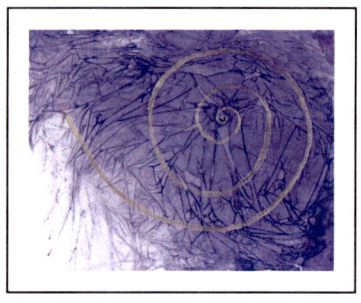

Forgive others,
Forgive situations
and,
most challenging of all
in this world,

Forgive yourself...

When you only Observe
and do not Judge,

You will see every past experience
Quietly,
Peacefully,
with all its amazing Richness
and Beauty.

You will then begin to close
your Golden Circles of
Experience.

Life is Beautiful

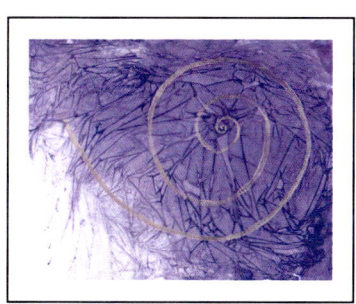

# These Golden Circles

are your personal patterns of belief
and behaviour...
which you keep repeating...

until you can Understand
what they were all about
and

Why you created them...

๑

To complete all your Circles
is to complete
your need for the incarnated
Journeying.

When you arrive
at that point, you will
Bless your Journeys
and truly
Know that

# Life is Beautiful

Your Golden Circles of Life
are simply
Beautiful

# Indigo Spirals

Lighting your amazing
Journey
back

Home

Life
is
Beautiful!

## With Grateful Thanks

To my wonderful partner, who helped me think more succinctly!

Without her wise words, I'd still be struggling to start writing.

Thank you, too, for listening to my interminable ramblings about how I was going to best illustrate the book!

Also to my friend Olivia, who read through the fourth draft and gave me such positive encouragement.

Thank you, too, for your time and insight in our brainstorming session for the extra eleven pages!

To my daughter, Lesley-Anne, who was such an invaluable help and patient listener while I was producing the artwork!

# An Explanation about Why I Called my Book Indigo Spirals

## Indigo

The colour given to the Third Eye chakra – the powerful energy centre located in the forehead. Indigo is the symbolic colour of spiritual attainment, self-mastery and wisdom.

The Brow or Third Eye chakra provides one with intuitive information outside the mind's store, accessing the knowledge we own as Divine beings.

This chakra (and the colour indigo) aids in accessing inner and outer vision.

The Third Eye is the doorway into the subconscious and can assist in releasing, and eliminating, negative, fearful aspects of the conscious and unconscious mind so that the 'higher' aspects of the human soul can be accessed.

The Brow chakra is directly related to the senses of sight and hearing, intelligence and psychic power.

It has to do with perception. It is the seat of understanding that affects how we see the world we live in and how we make sense of what is being perceived.

When this chakra is working properly, it can help remove confusion or indecision, thereby increasing the ability to see clearly and make important distinctions between that which is truly how things are, and that which appears to be real but has been created through fear and conditioning.

## Spirals

The spiral has been used as a highly complex symbol since the beginning of time. It has certainly been used since Palaeolithic times.

The spiral's meaning varies between cultures, but common interpretations are: evolution of the universe (time), continual change, spiritual growth and transformation, migrations, life, infinity and origins.

The spiral variously represents both solar and lunar powers, the air, the waters, rolling thunder and lightning. It is also a vortex, the great creative force, an emanation.

Some of the oldest examples of human art are depictions of spirals, painted or carved into rock, often found in burial sites.

From magnetic fields to vast galaxies swirling in space, spirals can be seen in every aspect of nature.

We see them in the physical forces which shape the Earth – the tides of the ocean, the winds of the atmosphere – and within life itself.

The spiral has left no human culture untouched and every aspect of human culture embraces the spiral.

As revolution, or 're-evolution', the spiral progression is symbolic of the transpersonal journey to that higher level of consciousness sought by all esoteric and occult systems. It is linked to the 'circle', the ancient symbol of the goddess, the womb, fertility, feminine serpent force, continual change and the evolution of the universe.

Spirals, or whorls, are associated with the spinning and weaving of the web of life and the veil of the Mother Goddess, controller of destiny and the weaver of the web of illusion.

As you look at a spiral, it appears to expand or contract. As such, it can depict the increase and decrease of the sun, or the waxing and waning of the moon, and so becomes an analogy of growth and expansion, death and contraction, winding and unwinding, birth and death.

It also can signify continuity: eternity.

The spiral portrays the revolving heavens, the course of the sun, the cyclic seasons and the rotation of the Earth.

As the whirl of the air in thunder and storms, and the movement of the waters, it denotes fertility and the dynamic aspect of creation – a spinning vortex of great generative force.

The spiral is also a symbol that corresponds to the underlying reality of nature, and has manifested itself in art, religion and philosophy from the earliest times.

Spiral energy fields are all around us and within us. They give pattern to our existence, from microcosm to macrocosm, determining structures from the tiny vortexes of subatomic particles and the DNA molecule to the awesome 'island universes' of galaxies where stars are born and the conditions for life are created.

The spiral form is integral to strength and growth and it may be that all curves of growth are based upon it.

The spiral curve is found in the tusks of elephants and warthogs, the teeth of beavers and rodents, claws of cats, beaks of birds, horns of sheep, the flight of birds, and in the arrangement of sunflower seeds in sunflowers.

It is found in magnetic fields, in the volutes of waves, the swirls of weather systems, the tides of the ocean, in green shoots of plants, and in human anatomy and embryos. Some animals, especially aquatic species, possess a twisting locomotion.

Fibres in the ventricles of the heart run in spiral lines so that the muscular constriction forcing the blood circulation is like the twist of a screw.

In the labyrinth of the inner ear, the cochlea, which analyses frequencies of sound and vibration, is shaped like a snail and consists of a spiral canal within which lies a smaller membranous spiral passage.

The spiral vortex is found in whirlpools in water and in the double helix structure of the DNA molecule. It is nature's most common form for the transmission of energy, radiating out and drawing in simultaneously, representing infinity and eternity.

Spirals are all around us in nature, such as the unfolding fern and sea shells.

In fact, one of the most beautiful manifestations of the spiral form is found in nature: the nautilus shell, a marine mollusc related to the squid. The biological principle that governs the growth of the mollusc's shell is the simplest possible: the size increases but the shape is unaltered. The mollusc's shell grows longer and wider to accommodate the growing animal, but the shell remains always similar to itself. It grows at one end only, each increment of length being balanced by a proportional increase of radius so that its form is unchanged. The shell grows by accretion of material; more accurately, it accumulates rather than grows.

It grows close to the proportion of the Golden Ratio used in the construction of sacred buildings including the pyramids at Giza and the Greek Parthenon. The Golden Ratio has been studied for centuries in mathematics and it revolutionised art in the fifteenth century.

Indeed, it has fascinated mathematicians for millennia, stimulated by the magical phenomenon of a shape that can grow in size without ever changing its form.

On the metaphysical plane, it symbolises the realms of existence, the various modalities of being, the wanderings of the soul in manifestation and the ultimate return to the centre: the Source of All Creation – the Ultimate Divine.

Our experience of habits created by the conditioning generated by our social structure and interaction are also in the form of circles and spirals.

As we continue to replay the same experiences, our consciousness follows the circle.

As we break free from the habitual re-enactment of those familiar practices, we are following the spiral: ever moving away from the source of those beliefs, fears and collusions with the perception of others, until we break free to be the powerful, creative, wonderful beings that we really are. The cycle of limitation is broken and reformed into the spiral of growth, creative generation and expansion, and limitless potential.

So, the spiral is a powerful symbol that is found in cultures all over the world and is reflected in shamanism, serpent cults, dragon lore, geomancy, mysticism, and ritual art and dance. The spiral represents dynamic growth and metamorphosis, the vortex, an opening or reawakening, and the movement or oscillation between the dualities of the physical and the spiritual.

The archetypal image of the spiral represents a path that could be climbed in stages to reach God – the Divine Source – and our own Divine Being-ness.

It is a symbol of the spiritual journey towards the divine essence within all of us – a map of the soul's progression through life's experiences.

The spiral symbolises the fusion and flow of dynamic opposites balanced in universal harmony, as represented in the yin-yang symbol.

The Kundalini – the Sanskrit word for spiral – rises through the body through the chakras on the central meridian line of the body to activate spiritual and psychic energy. The Kundalini is often depicted as a coiled, sleeping serpent, resting at the base of the spine, poised to spring up through the body at times of great spiritual growth.

Today, the spiral still runs deep within our culture. It forms the logos of a large number of companies and has come to symbolise magic, dreams, desires and, most importantly, eternity.

It is perhaps this never-ending quality of the spiral which intrigues and draws us so greatly. When a spiral is drawn or made using paper and then turned, it creates the illusion that it is twisting forever away or towards us. The repetitive animation of a twisting spiral also evokes deep relaxation and calm, which accounts for the spiral's close association with the art of hypnotism. In some cases, people even create spirals themselves in order to ease the constantly active mind. If a person is left to 'doodle' on a piece of paper in a relaxed state, it is very likely that they will draw spirals and swirls as their subconscious mind controls the pen.

The word spiral comes from the Latin 'spiralis' or 'spira' and the Greek 'speira', meaning spire or coil, or a conical or pyramidal structure. It is also from the Latin 'spirare', meaning to breathe, expire and inspire, and has ancient roots in ideas of creation, life-giving and aspiration.

The word Spirit is similar in origin, representing the animating divine element of life and reason. Spirit stands for the vital, fundamental principle of existence, as well as for qualities such as courage, strength and vivacity of mind.

The spiral is the way of the universe, the link between microcosm and macrocosm, science and spirituality.

It is the sign of the eternal, creative and organising principle at work in the Universe, the Pattern of our Earthly life experience and spiritual development.

The spiral is a key to existence and the inner essence of reality.

The word

'spiral'

is within the word

'spiritual'

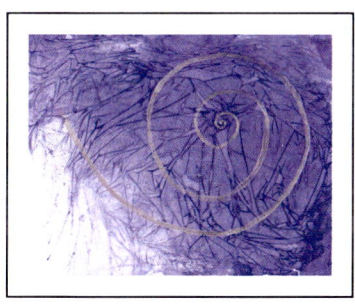

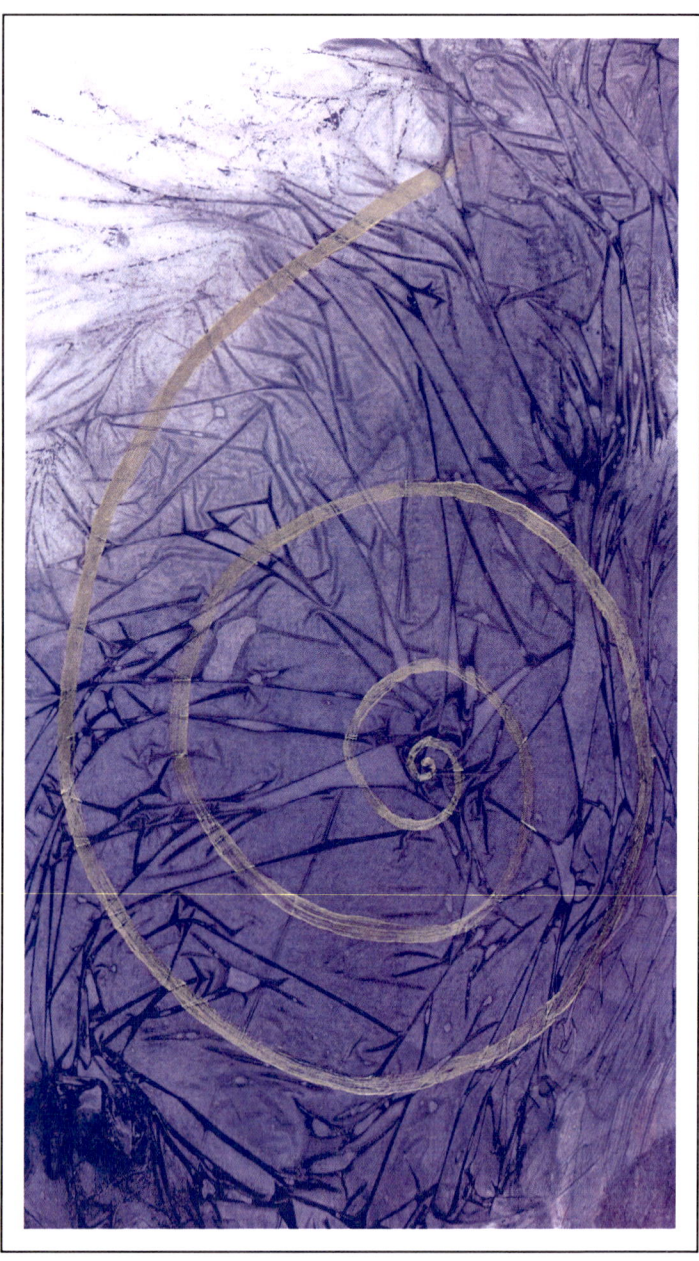

VIRGINNIA RADFORD currently lives in Newbury, Berkshire, England; and is the single parent of three beautiful, now grown-up, children.

She has been a lecturer and teacher of art and mathematics at secondary-school level, finally coming out of teaching in 2006 to fully concentrate upon developing her spiritual work.

Virginnia is a self-taught artist who took an art course almost by accident at Teacher Training College for, although she had always wanted to teach, she had no idea which subject she preferred – she simply enjoyed them all (except needlework and home economics)! She has a B.ed art degree from Bristol University.

Although a natural psychic since birth, she became more aware of her abilities when called by Spirit to begin training as a healer in 1993.

She became a registered healer with the National Federation of Spiritual Healers in 1995, and a Reiki master in 1999; and is an internationally and nationally recognised and respected psychic artist, spiritual counsellor and psychic.

Virginnia is a spiritual/energy healer, shamanic healer, and has many years' experience in running psychic development courses and meditation groups. As a psychic, she offers channelled readings, soul journey contract readings and psychic art.

For further information please visit:
www.starlightangel.co.uk